MODS

HACKS FOR MINECRAFTERS

THE UNOFFICIAL GUIDE TO TIPS AND TRICKS THAT OTHER GUIDES WON'T TEACH YOU

MEGAN MILLER

BLOOMSBURY

LONDON OXFORD NEW YORK NEW DELHI SYDNEY

First published 2017 by Bloomsbury Publishing Plc
50 Bedford Square, London, WC1B 3DP

www.bloomsbury.com

Bloomsbury is a registered trademark of Bloomsbury Publishing Plc

Copyright © 2017 Bloomsbury Publishing Plc
Text copyright © 2017 Megan Miller
Minecraft® is a registered trademark of Notch Development AB.
The Minecraft game is copyright © Mojang AB.

The rights of Megan Miller to be identified as the author of this work respectively have been asserted by
them in accordance with the Copyrights Designs and Patents Act 1988.

ISBN 978-1-4088-9596-2

A CIP catalogue for this book is available from the British Library.

All internet addresses given in this book were correct at the time of going to press. The author and
publishers regret any inconvenience caused if addresses have changed or if websites have ceased to
exist, but can accept no responsibility for any such changes.

Printed in China by Leo Paper Products, Heshan, Guangdong

1 3 5 7 9 10 8 6 4 2

REMEMBER THAT SOME DOWNLOADS CAN DISGUISE MALWARE,
WHICH WILL CAUSE DAMAGE TO YOUR DEVICE. ALWAYS MAKE SURE
YOU ARE DOWNLOADING FROM REPUTABLE SOURCES.

TABLE OF CONTENTS

CHAPTER 1

ALL ABOUT MODS

Welcome to the mad, magical, and high-tech world of modded Minecraft. Modded Minecraft isn't a single game, it's Minecraft modified with the mods you want to play with. You can play with one mod, or a couple of mods, a dozen mods, or a mod-pack that comes ready with a preset selection of mods.

What Are Mods?

"Mod" is short for "modification", and mods are game programming objects that change the way a game behaves. In Minecraft, mods can change how you farm, how you fight, how you mine, how (and what) you craft, and more. Some mods are simple and change just one small part of the game. For example, JourneyMap adds a very handy mapping system to Minecraft. Other mods change major aspects of Minecraft. The magical mod Thaumcraft creates a unique type of sorcery, with spells, wands, magic energy, and magical mobs for you to play with. Some more examples are:

- **Simply Jetpacks** lets you craft powered jetpacks to fly around in your world. (This is probably my favorite mod – there's nothing better than flying!)

- **The Twilight Forest** creates an entirely new dimension you can visit by travelling through a special portal. The Twilight Forest dimension has new animals, mobs, boss mobs, dungeons, and more to explore.

- **The Extra Utilities** adds a bunch of interesting and useful items, tools, and blocks, like conveyor belts, to help move captured mobs or items around, and a bunch of power generators for early game power.

The Twilight Forest mod adds an entirely new dimension to explore, with new boss mobs, biomes, and more.

Mods are made for the PC version of Minecraft, and there are several places you can find them:

- Planet Minecraft (PMC) at planetminecraft.com/resources/mods/

- The Minecraft Forum at minecraftforum.net/forums/mapping-and-modding/minecraft-mods

- Curse at curse.com/mc-mods/minecraft

- Mod authors' websites

What Are Modpacks?

Modpacks are collections of mods that are carefully selected to work together, both in balanced gameplay and in technical compatibility. Modpacks are the easiest way to get started playing with mods, because they are easy to download and install. Some modpacks come with a questing system that gives you challenges to accomplish – and sometimes rewards when you complete them. Some modpacks have an overall theme or storyline. In the Crash Landing modpack, you are stranded on an unknown planet with a dying spaceship and must battle a very harsh desert environment.

In the classic Crash Landing modpack, you are stranded on a dusty planet and must struggle to survive against a harsh, dry landscape.

You can find and install modpacks using modpack launchers. The most popular modpack launchers are:

- Feed the Beast (FTB) Launcher. The Feed the Beast team has produced and gathered a large set of modpacks, along with a launcher, which you can find at their site feed-the-beast.com.

- Curse Launcher. The gaming network site has also created a launcher, Curse for Minecrafters, that incorporates Feed the Beast modpacks and others, which you can find at beta.cursevoice.com/games/minecraft. (This launcher is also used for Curse's voice chat application.)

- ATLauncher, available at atlauncher.com.

- Technic Launcher, available at technicpack.net.

Modpack launchers, like the Curse launcher, make installing modpacks easy.

This book will look at some of the most popular mods and mod-packs available and show you how to download them. I'll also show you how to get started playing with modpacks. Many of these mods offer so much gameplay that it is likely you'll want even more information on them. You can visit several websites to get more information on how to play. Visit the Curse Minecraft mods site (curse.com/mc-mods/minecraft), the Minecraft Forum (minecraftforum.net). The FTB wiki (ftbwiki.org) and forums (forum.feed-the-beast.com/forum/) are also a great source of information about many mods. Many mods have deeper explanations at their own wiki sites. You can also visit my website at meganfmiller.com for links to these sites and helpful YouTube videos that look at how to play with these mods.

Warning: Mods can change the original Minecraft programming code and you have to be very careful backing up your worlds and installing them. Mods are unsupported by Mojang, the game developers. Even though Mojang has made Minecraft so that it can be modded, if you run into a problem, Mojang can't help you. You'll have to rely on the community of modders and players to help you through technical and gameplay problems.

BEFORE YOU START INSTALLING AND PLAYING WITH MODS, THERE ARE SOME CONCEPTS YOU SHOULD BE FAMILIAR WITH:

Minecraft Versions

Mods are always a little bit behind vanilla Minecraft. (Vanilla Minecraft is the term that people use to describe playing Minecraft without any mods.) That's because the mod developers must wait till a new stable release of Minecraft is released before they can even begin adapting their existing mods or creating new mods for it. Currently, several mods are available for Minecraft 1.8, but the bulk of mods and modpacks are running on Minecraft 1.7.10.

If you install mods or modpacks individually, you will need to be aware of what version of Minecraft they work with. If you are manually installing mods, you will need to download the right version of Minecraft as well. If you choose to use a custom launcher or modpack launcher, this will be taken care of for you fairly seamlessly. A custom or modpack launcher replaces the Minecraft launcher. (When you run Minecraft, the first window that appears is the Minecraft launcher, not the game itself.) You can use the Minecraft launcher to make and edit game-play profiles, and each profile can have different settings for the version of Minecraft you play, the amount of RAM memory it uses, and more.

Mod Makers and Downloads

Mods are created by Minecraft fans who come up with an idea for something they'd like to see in Minecraft, program it into a mod, and release the mod for players to freely download and use in their own game. Unlike programmers at Mojang and other game companies, mod authors don't have a full support team helping them. This means that it isn't unusual for bugs to slip through in the programming, so you have to be careful to make backups of worlds you don't want to lose.

Many mod developers make a little bit of money from advertisments that are placed on the download sites they use. If you use a mod developer's site to download a mod, you need to keep an eye out for the advertisements. The advertisements often look like they are the real links to the mod but may instead download unwanted software to your PC. If you are taken to an AdFly website for the download, wait for the timer on the top right to count down and then click the **Skip Ad** button on the top right. Because it can be very difficult to tell the difference between an advertisement and the real download link, I recommend downloading the mod if possible from Curse first, and then donating (if your parents agree) a small amount to the mod author directly.

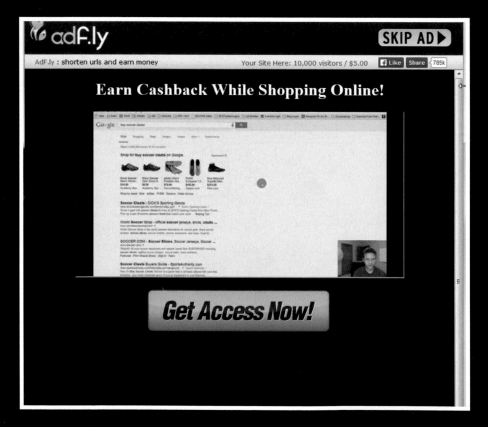

When you download individual mods, you are likely to come across web pages that are loaded with advertisements that look like download links. Be careful. With AdFly sites, like this one, you want to wait several seconds until the **Skip Ad** button appears at the top right, then click that.

You can also help mod developers by signing up to be a beta tester. The Minecraft Forum, at minecraftforum.net, is a central location to discover mods that have been released and are still being worked on. Developers will post announcements here saying that they are looking for beta testers for their mod.

Backups

Mods work by changing some of the programming code in Minecraft. There are thousands of mods, and often mods do not work well with each other. And there are mods that can corrupt your world.

All of this means that if you are manually installing mods (and even if you're not), regularly back up your worlds. To do this, go to your Minecraft game directory and make a backup of the folder named **saves**. In the 'saves' folder are all the files for each world you play. In Windows, this folder is typically located at C:\Users\Megan\AppData\Roaming\minecraft. If you have trouble finding the 'saves' folder, start the Minecraft launcher and click **Edit Profile**. In the Edit Profile window, click the **Open Game Dir** button at the bottom to open your Minecraft directory.

The files for your Minecraft worlds are in your Minecraft game directory's **saves** folder. You can copy the entire folder to another location to back it up.

Modded Multiplayer

This book looks at playing mods in single-player worlds. However, you can find servers that offer modded play. In modded multiplayer, both the server and the client (you) must have mods installed. Most modded multiplayer servers use one of the popular modpacks, such as a Feed the Beast modpack or the Tekkit modpack (available from the Technic launcher).

Getting Technical Help

As I mentioned earlier, mod developers work and distribute their mods for free. They don't have teams of developers and other support to help them, so they can't provide support to users the same way large gaming companies like EA (Electronic Arts) can do. They also can't debug their work against every possible scenario. If you are having technical or gameplay difficulties, there are several places to look for help. In addition to the sites mentioned earlier, look at the mod's page at Planet Minecraft (planetminecraft.com) and at Curse (curse.com/mc-mods/minecraft). Check to see if you have downloaded the right versions and all required mods, and look for any troubleshooting FAQs or discussion forums at the mod author's website. The community message board site reddit.com also has a large community of Minecraft players who might have already discussed the same problems. Of course, you can also try searching Google with your specific problem, such as "Minecraft Twilight Forest portal not working".

CHAPTER 2

INSTALLING MODS

There are three main ways to install mods:

1. Individually, using the Forge mod (not recommended except for advanced computer users).

2. Individually, using a custom launcher.

3. As packs of mods, using a modpack launcher (recommended).

First, a key concept in installing mods is making sure you use a separate instance of Minecraft for mods. An instance of Minecraft is a full and separate installation of Minecraft, including the main Minecraft program file, the minecraft.jar file, and any related files and folders for worlds, resource packs, and more. Using separate instances means that any problems a mod causes will be limited to affecting the single instance it is used in.

Manual/Forge Installation

Forge is a very widely used mod that is used to install and manage mods. It also provides an application programming interface (API) that helps modders create mods. An API is a set of programming tools for working with a specific program. All of this means that mods using Forge tend to work well together. You need to install Forge in order to use any of the Forge-created mods.

However, what Forge doesn't do is automatically create new instances of Minecraft, and this means that your Minecraft application is vulnerable to being corrupted accidentally by a mod, so I won't recommend installing mods individually using Forge unless you have advanced computer skills.

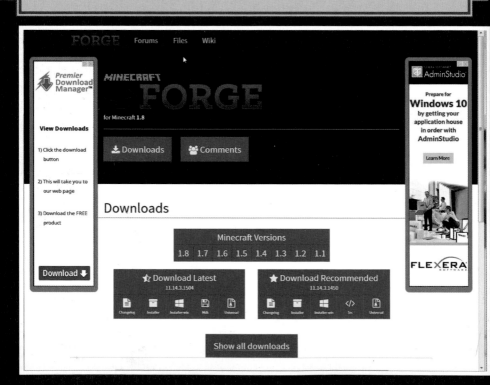

Forge is the mod that allows lots of mods to work well together. If you are downloading Forge manually, you need to make sure you are getting the right version for the version of Minecraft you will use.

Basically, the Forge process is to download and run the Minecraft Forge installer from files.minecraftforge.net and then place zipped mod files that you have downloaded into your mods folder. The mods folder is located in your Minecraft game directory. But, as I've said, if you are new to mods or aren't an advanced computer user, I don't recommend this, as it is very easy to get something wrong, both in downloading and in installation.

Installing Mods with a Custom Launcher

You can use a custom launcher like MultiMC to help create and manage mods. You still need to find and download mods individually, but the launcher will help you separate modded worlds from each other and from your vanilla worlds. You still need to maintain caution when downloading mods, both to avoid fake advertising downloads and infected files. If you're ready for this, you can follow the instructions for working with the MultiMC launcher in the Appendix.

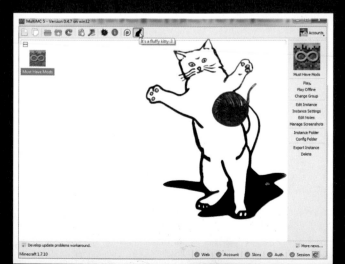

The MultiMC launcher helps you create different instances of Minecraft, but you still need to download mods individually.

Installing modpacks with a modpack launcher is the easiest way by far to start playing with Minecraft mods, and this is what I recommend for beginning modded gameplay. All you do, basically, is download and run the modpack launcher. When you start the launcher, you can select which modpack you want to play with, and the launcher will install the mods and create the directories and Minecraft instances you need to keep everything working and separate.

In addition, there are strong communities that maintain the top modpack launchers, and along with forums and documentation, it is easier to find help for technical issues when you are using a modpack launcher.

Four of the most popular modpack launchers are the Curse Launcher, the ATLauncher, the Feed the Beast (FTB) Launcher, and the Technic Launcher. They are all free to use. Each of these modpack launchers have different modpacks you can install, although some modpacks appear in several launchers. The FTB modpacks are being integrated into the Curse Launcher, so you will find the FTB modpacks in the Curse Launcher. In all of these launchers you will find settings to adjust the RAM memory used and the initial game window size. They will also keep your Minecraft instances separate and allow you to install vanilla Minecraft as well, so that you can use the launcher for all your Minecraft games. You will also need to add your Minecraft game profile to each launcher so that it can verify your account.

Installing the Curse Launcher (PC)

1. Go to the Curse website (curse.com) and download the Curse for Minecraft installer (beta.cursevoice.com/games/minecraft).

2. When the download is complete, run the installer.

3. When the launcher is finished installing, run the launcher. You will need to register a new Curse account if you don't already have one.

4. To open the Minecraft areas of the launcher, click the **Minecraft** tab at the top. If you are prompted to install additional items on this tab as shown, do so.

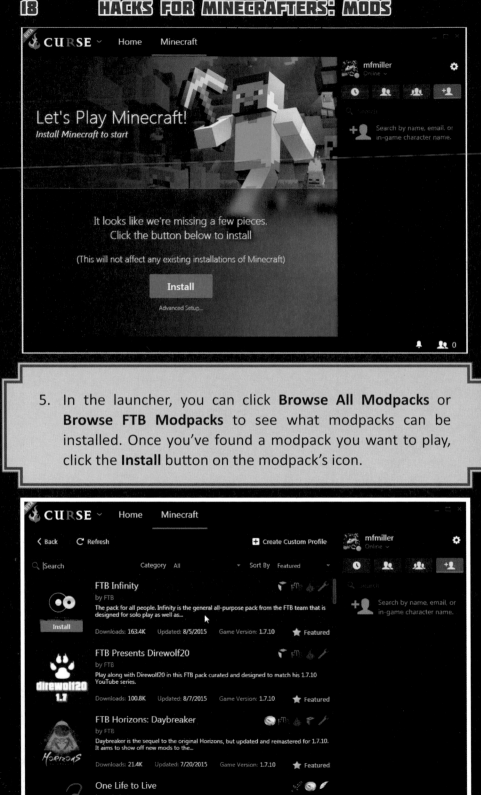

5. In the launcher, you can click **Browse All Modpacks** or **Browse FTB Modpacks** to see what modpacks can be installed. Once you've found a modpack you want to play, click the **Install** button on the modpack's icon.

Installing the FTB Launcher (PC and Mac)

1. Go to the Feed the Beast website (feed-the-beast.com) and click **Download Now** on the home page. Download the .jar or .exe files for PC or the .jar file for Mac.

2. Run the .exe or .jar file after it is downloaded to run the installer. It will download the base files you need and automatically open the FTB launcher for you.

3. In the launcher, you can click the **FTB modpacks** or the **3rd party modpacks** tab at the top to browse modpacks available. You will need to add your Minecraft game profile using the **Create Profile** button.

4. When you've selected a modpack you'd like to play, click **Launch** to download the files and play the modpack. For very large modpacks, it may take some time to download all the files.

You install other launchers, like the ATLauncher and the Technic Launcher in pretty much the same way. Download the installer or launcher app and run it. In the launcher, you can select which modpack you want to run. When you start or select the modpack for the first time, the modpack's files will download. You'll find the ATLauncher at atlauncher.com and the Technic Launcher at technicpack.net.

CHAPTER 3

MUST-HAVE MODS

Everyone playing modded Minecraft has their favourite mods. But there are some mods you feel like you can't play without, once you've experienced their genius. The must-have mods below are favourites of mine and many other Minecrafters. They are some of the most-downloaded mods and are often included in modpacks.

These must-haves fix common Minecraft annoyances or frustrations, or make things simpler in a modded world. Have you ever forgotten where that desert village is? Or wasted too much time waiting for a large oak's leaf blocks to despawn? Can't remember that recipe for an enchantment table? These mods solve those little irks and more.

Not Enough Items (NEI)

Author: chicken_bones

Not Enough Items (NEI) transforms the inventory interface you get when you press **E** in Minecraft. It gives you an overlay of all the blocks and items available in Minecraft and any installed mods. You can page through or search the list.

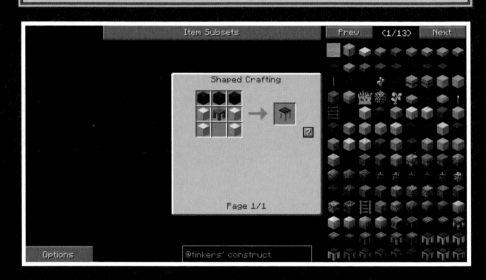

To search for all the items a mod adds, type @ and the mod name in the search box.

The brilliance of NEI is that you can easily find recipes for any item, as well as any recipes an item is used in. If you hover over an item in NEI's interface and press **R**, NEI will show you the crafting recipe for that item. If you make the item in a smelter or other contraption (like getting stone from smelting cobble), NEI will show that as well. And if you press **U**, NEI will show you the recipes that the item is used in.

This is great for vanilla Minecraft, but in modded Minecraft, where you can have thousands of craftable items with different recipes and machines, it's a must.

What's especially awesome is this: if you are working with the crafting table, NEI can automatically fill the grid with ingredients you need. To do this, you have to find the recipe in NEI, select it, and then shift-click the question mark beside the recipe. If you have the crafting ingredients in your personal inventory, NEI will fill the crafting grid with the ingredients so you can just drag your crafted item immediately from the grid. To fill the crafting grid with previews of what's needed, simply click the question mark.

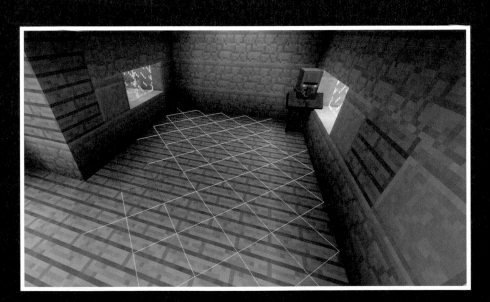

Another fantastic feature of NEI is the mob-spawning indicator. Press **F7** and blocks will be highlighted with a yellow X if a mob can spawn there at night and a red X if a mob can spawn at any time. This lets you know exactly where to put torches or other lights.

NEI has become such a staple that modders have created additional add-on mods, like NEI Integration and NEI Add-ons, that help with crafting recipes from other mods.

In NEI World options, you can play in a cheat mode that allows you to access any item. You can also use buttons for changing the weather, setting the time of day, and the "magnet". The magnet lets any objects you accidentally drop zoom back to your inventory.

Simply Jetpacks

Author: tonius111

Jetpacks are a great way to avoid the somewhat nastier mobs you'll often find in modded Minecraft.

When I start a modded world, one of my first goals, after setting up a base, food resources, and a mining operation, is to obtain a jetpack. Having a jetpack, for me, means I feel much safer. I can fly away from any monster that surprises me, take a moment to breathe, and then kill it or figure out my escape. This is a massive boon in the Nether, which, in a modpack, might be much more dangerous than the vanilla Nether. A jetpack also makes it easier to build neater structures. And, of course, jetpacks are awesome by themselves.

Simply Jetpacks is actually an add-on mod for another popular tech mod, Thermal Expansion, which itself works with the mods Thermal Foundation and CoHCore (a code library), so you'll have to have those three mods installed together. These mods add ores and ore-processing machines to Minecraft. They're pretty essential, too, and we'll look at them in the Tech Mods chapter.

To craft a jetpack, you do need some resources and special machines to replenish its energy – so it doesn't feel like cheating! The lowest level jetpack is within your reach after a trip to the Nether and gathering some resources (a variety of fairly common materials: ores, glass, sulfur, redstone, etc.).

To run the jetpacks added by Simply Jetpacks, you'll need the energetic infuser machine from Thermal Expansion to replenish its energy. You'll also need a power source for the infuser, like this survivalist generator from Extra Utilities.

Fast Leaf Decay

Author: Olafski

No more waiting for the leaves of your chopped tree to despawn. Chop the tree and the leaves crumble within seconds. This is a small mod that does one thing perfectly. Beware, though – once you have got used to fast leaf decay, it's very hard to go back to vanilla.

Chop down a tree and its leaves disappear almost immediately with the Fast Leaf Decay mod.

Inventory Tweaks

Author: Kobata

With Inventory Tweaks, when you open a chest, you can click the buttons at the top to sort the contents. Press the ellipses button to open up Inventory Tweaks options.

Like Waila and NEI, Inventory Tweaks adds some incredibly useful functions to inventories. Automatic refill means that when you are using blocks, like placing cobble to make a wall, and your stack runs out of that block, your inventory slot will automatically refill with more of the block (if it is somewhere in your inventory). Repair-friendly refill means that if your pick breaks, its inventory slot will refill with the same type of pick (if you have one in inventory).

In Inventory Tweaks options, you can turn on and off auto-refill and repair-friendly refill.

Author: squeek502

Waila (What Am I Looking At) is a small mod that gives you information about blocks. It will tell you the name of the block you are looking at and what mod it is from. This may seem fairly useless in vanilla Minecraft, but in a modpack with hundreds of mods, each with new blocks and items, it's extremely helpful.

Waila shows you the name of the object you're looking at and the mod it is from.

If you also install the add-on mod Waila Harvestability, it will tell you the best tool to use to break the block in front of you. This is a huge help when you are working with the more complex tiers of tools of Tinkers' Construct.

With Waila Harvestability mod, you'll also see what tool you can use to harvest the block.

Tinkers' Construct

Authors: mDiyo, jadedcat, boniasboni

Tinkers' Construct (also referred to as Tinkers or tcon) overhauls the tool and weapon system of Minecraft. It has become such a staple in modded Minecraft that you will find it in many modpacks.

With Tinkers, you have many more choices than wood, iron, gold, or diamond to make your tools and weapons from. Tinkers adds new ores to the Overworld, like aluminium, copper, and tin, as well as a few new ores to the Nether, like ardite and cobalt. It also adds some gravel forms of ores.

This Tinkers' pick is made from a manyullyn pickaxe head (purple), a paper rod, and a pink slime binding. Extra effects are added with a ball of moss for autorepair (green), speed with redstone, and luck (fortune) with lapis.

With Tinkers' Construct, you can find gravel versions of ores in the open as well as underground. To work with the ores, and cast them into weapon parts, you first make a smeltery. A smeltery will melt the ores you put inside and also allows you to create special alloys from combinations of ores. Once melted, you pour out your metals in basins, to get blocks of a metal, or into casts, to make weapon and tool parts or ingots.

To melt ores, you'll have to make a smeltery. You can find the beginnings of a smeltery in villages.

Tinkers' tools don't disappear when their durability is used up. Instead, they "break" and stop working. You can then repair them using one or more ingots or units of their base material, like iron or gold.

There's a huge variety of Tinkers' weapons and tools. In addition to regular Minecraft tools, you can make different types of swords, daggers, broadaxes, lumber axes, scythes, crossbows, and more. Out of these, my current favourites are the hammer, which you use like a pick, to mine a 3x3 hole, and the excavator, which mines sand, gravel, and dirt, also in 3x3 blocks. These two tools make manual mining a very sweet and speedy activity.

Tinkers' Construct also adds some slime to your world: small slime sky islands made of slime dirt and slime grass, and purple and green congealed slime, with slime trees and blue slime mobs. Occasionally a King Slime boss mob will spawn and jump over the island edge to fall into your neighbourhood. The King Slime has 100 health points and will sometimes drop the rare King Slime Hammer, a decent weapon that can deal 7 hearts of damage.

A slime sky island added with the Tinkers' mod.

JourneyMap

Author: TechMap

JourneyMap adds a small map to your Minecraft game window and a large map screen you can access by pressing **J**. The maps show not only where you are, but also any mobs that are nearby. Underground, it will show features like lava and water. You can configure JourneyMap, from the map size and zoom level, to see which mobs it shows.

JourneyMap adds a small map to the top left. It also lets you add waypoints, which appear on your screen as beams of light.

Best of all, you can add waypoints, a type of in-game bookmark, to your world. A waypoint places a coloured beam of light in the world at your choice of location, and you can name the waypoints to remember what they mark. To quickly set a waypoint, press **B**. You can see waypoints from far away, and labels show the waypoint name and how far away they are. This is perfect for marking your portal in the Nether.

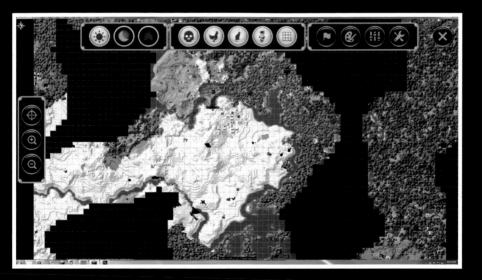

Press **J** to see JourneyMap's full-screen map, where you can also adjust settings and access the list of waypoints you have created.

Extra Utilities

Author: RWTema

The Extra Utilities mod is a collection of assorted items and blocks that can be extremely useful, from early game power generators and pipes that are easy to craft, to conveyor belts and spikes that can be used to create mob traps. Some of the top, for me, are:

- Golden Bag of Holding. This bag lets you carry a double-chest's worth of more stuff in your personal inventory.

- Builder's Wand. The Builder's Wand lets you place 8 blocks at a time, of whatever block it is pointing at, in the next layer in the wand's direction. You do need to have enough matching blocks in your inventory. The Super Builder's Wand can place up to 49 blocks.

- Angel Block. The Angel Block can be placed anywhere in the world, for example, in mid-air, so you can easily start a construction in the sky without having to build a column first.

The conveyor belts from Extra Utilities make it very easy to force mobs into your mob grinder.

Optifine

Author: sp614x

If there's one mod that vanilla players use, it's Optifine. It's a utility mod that improves the Minecraft fps, or framerate (how fast the game runs), as well as visuals. It improves lighting and how textures connect, and gives many more options under the Minecraft Visual Settings screen. There are three versions – Lite, Standard, and Ultra. The version that is designed to work best with other mods is Standard.

CHAPTER 4

MODS FOR ADVENTURE AND RPG

Mods for adventure and RPG (role-playing games) add new biomes and dimensions to explore. Some of these mods change the way villages and villagers behave, and others bring fantastic new flora and fauna to your Minecraft world. These are a few of the most popular; they all work with Forge, and you'll find many in popular modpacks like FTB Infinity.

Biomes O' Plenty

Author: Glitchfiend

You can explore over 70 new biomes with the Biomes O' Plenty mod – from Alps and Badlands to Tropical Rainforest and Wetlands. In addition to giving us new flowers, shrubs, even new dirt varieties, the mod adds over 20 types of trees that grow in the biomes, like bamboo trees and giant redwood trees. These new trees are also great for builders, as their logs give lots of new colour options for wood planks, stairs, and slabs.

Watch out for the quicksand added by Biomes O' Plenty (although it can work out in your favour, as it can trap mobs as well). It's slightly darker than ordinary sand, and it can suffocate you. To get out of quicksand, move to the edge and break the quicksand blocks beneath you.

A few biomes are magical, such as the Mystic Grove biome, with magic trees and glowflowers. The Biomes O' Plenty mod also includes five new biomes in the Nether, including the Boneyard (the first image in this chapter). In the Boneyard, you can find gravestones and giant bones sticking out of the netherrack.

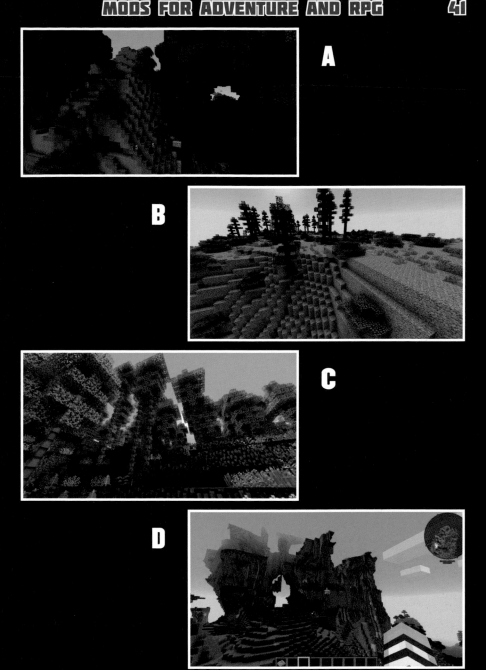

Biomes O' Plenty biomes include Sacred Springs (A), Canyon (B), Bamboo Forest (C), and Jade Cliffs (D).

Tip: To use this mod, you need to create a new Minecraft world with its World Type set to Biomes O' Plenty.

Mo' Creatures

Author: DrZhark

This mod adds over 40 animal and hostile monster mobs to your game, including birds, insects, ocean life, big golems, wraiths, werewolves, and the dragonlike wyverns. You'll have to build your own zoo though! Some of the mobs can be tamed and kept as pets, and others – like the elephants – you can also ride.

Mo' Creatures adds passive and hostile mobs to the game, including big cats, foxes, elephants, and raccoons.

JurassiCraft

- - - - - - - - - -

Authors: kashmoney360, JTGhawk137, LieutenantGhost, TheDurp)Daedric

Get your prehistoric on with this mod inspired by the Jurassic Park movies. First, you'll have to mine to find the fossils and amber for dino DNA. Then you'll need to craft some specialized machines: a DNA extractor to get that ancient DNA and a cultivator to create the precious dino eggs.

These are the dinosaur fossil blocks you have to mine in order to create dinosaurs.

There are over 30 prehistoric creatures here, from the giant brachiosaurus, triceratops, raptors, and T. rex, to dodos and coelacanths. If you are dino mad, you might also want to try out another prehistoric creatures mod, Fossils and Archaeology Revival.

JurassiCraft adds dozens of dinosaurs, many of which you can tame and ride.

Twilight Forest

Author: Benimatic

If you like to explore new lands, fight powerful and strange mobs, and find hidden loot and treasure, Twilight Forest may be the mod for you. This very popular mod adds an entirely new enchanted and eerie dimension, similar to the Nether or the End. The Twilight Forest is crammed with adventurous content: new biomes, dungeons, mazes, castles, animals, boss mobs, trees, insects, and more.

The Twilight Forest adds an entirely new dimension that is permanently dusk.

The mobs, structures, and plants in Twilight Forest are all beautifully created and just exploring the land is an awesome experience. To get there, all you need to do is make a 2x2 hole, fill it with water, surround it with flowers, and throw in a diamond. After a few moments and a bang, the water pool will turn into your portal to the Twilight Forest. If you are going alone, make sure you have enchanted armour, weapons, and potions because some of the mobs in the Twilight Forest are quite powerful.

Mystcraft

Author: XCompWiz

The Mystcraft mod is inspired by the Myst series of video games and books. In Mystcraft, you write, or craft, enchanted books to create and travel to new worlds called Ages. You can create random Ages by creating a book with a blank page, or you can customize a new Age by including pages that describe a feature of the world. World features range from the type and organization of biomes to the colour of skies, types of ores, and more.

In Mystcraft, you create new worlds by crafting a mystical book using your writing desk.

Random Ages have a high chance of being unstable or dangerous. An unstable world has negative effects, like poisoning, spontaneous explosions, or decay, which makes the Age self-destruct.

Clicking on a descriptive book transports you to a platform in the new world.

You start by creating a descriptive book to create an Age. To travel to that Age, right-click on the book to open it and click on the black square. Be careful, because without a linking book back to the Overworld, or a sky fissure (a natural portal), you can get permanently stuck in your world.

To find pages with world features, locate the libraries in your new world. Inside are lecterns with new pages, and a hidden chest.

Minecraft Comes Alive

Author: WildBamaBoy

Minecraft Comes Alive (MCA) brings new life to your villages. Gone are the dour and bald villagers; in are new male and female villagers wearing player-like skins and assigned different personalities. They'll greet you in chat and you can right-click on them to bring up a whole new set of interactions, including chat, joke, gift, trade, hire, and more.

MCA populates your villages with a new assortment of villagers who you can "talk" with, give gifts to, and even marry.

Depending on your choosing an appropriate interaction with a villager (hint: don't joke too much with a serious character), you'll gain relationship points (hearts) with the villager, up to five red hearts that can improve to five gold hearts. After you've earned enough hearts, you can give a villager a crafted engagement ring, and then a crafted wedding ring. Once you're married, you can "procreate" for a baby item. After ten minutes, right-click the baby item and you'll have a child. What's great about the children is that you can assign them chores, like farming or fishing. They may whine, but if they have the right tools and items, they'll do it!

When you first start a world with MCA, you'll be given a crystal ball in your inventory. To begin your adventure, right-click the crystal ball to enter a library room, and you'll be given a choice of how to start with MCA. Start with a ready-made family (spouse and 0–2 kids), living in a village, living alone, or none of the above. You can also bypass the crystal ball, or choose none of the above and wait until you're ready to find a village and start interacting.

CHAPTER 5

MODS O' MAGIC

Minecraft's magical mods show how creative the Minecraft community is. Each of the four main magical mods – Thaumcraft, Botania, Witchery, and Blood Magic – bring a different system of magic to your world, with their own unique contraptions and ways to enhance your world with special effects and powers. These are all beautifully designed mods with excellent animations, objects, items, and gameplay.

Thaumcraft

Author: azanor

Thaumcraft is the ultimate magical Minecraft mod. It opens up hours of new gameplay as you learn the art of sorcery. You begin by making a simple wand, your guidebook (the Thaumonomicon), and a special device – the Thaumometer. With the Thaumometer, you can see and research the magical energy (essentia) present in all items and blocks, as well as find the magical energy nodes in the world around you.

Thaumcraft's Goggles of Revealing will show you where magical energy nodes are in the Minecraft world.

In Thaumcraft, you use the Thaumometer to research what magical aspects make up each item and object.

You have to research the right Minecraft blocks and items in order to progress in the Thaumcraft world, and there is a mini-game in a research table to help you learn more. As you gain more knowledge, more and more of Thaumcraft's magical recipes, abilities, and crafting will open up to you. You will be able to infuse objects with magical abilities at your Infusion Altar, distill potent energies from common blocks, and much more.

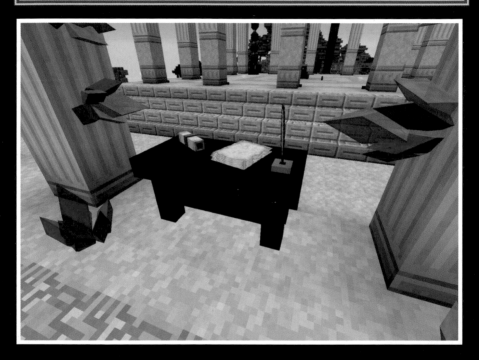

You can research new knowledge (of magical blocks, procedures, contraptions) by playing a mini-game using the research table.

Thaumcraft adds new trees, plants, ores, wands, cauldrons, staves, and contraptions. Especially fun are the golems – little utility mobs you can program to perform simple tasks for you, like planting trees or keeping your cauldron full of bubbling water.

The Infusion Altar allows you to infuse ordinary objects with magical essence to create new magical tools and items.

The popular mod Witchery opens up a more plant-based type of magic. Instead of working with natural energies, the way Thaumcraft does, Witchery uses the magical power of the plants around you. You can make small dolls called 'poppets' to protect you and write glyphs in a circle to perform magical rites. You'll have a witch's oven, cauldron, spinning wheel, altar, and brewing kettle to craft your potent charms. You can even bind a cat, owl, or toad to you to become your familiar, making you even more powerful.

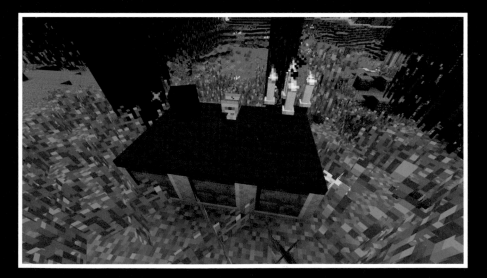

The Witchery altar gains power from the trees and plants around it.

Witchery is a complex and deep mod, creating a world of play with covens, werewolves, vampires, curses, spirits, and more. It adds larger villages to your world that are often walled. In these larger villages you can find several books to guide you in Witchery skills at bookshops, as well as witchcraft ingredients at the apothecary.

Witchery adds many mobs, one of which is the winged monkey which you can tame and have fight alongside you.

Larger, walled villages are also added by Witchery.

Blood Magic

Author: Way of Time

Blood Magic sounds gruesome, and it kind of is. It's also a fantastic mod, if you don't take the "blood" idea too seriously. Think of it as "life essence". With this mod, you take the health points of yourself and mobs, store it as a type of energy in an altar and orbs, and use it to create magical instruments, effects, and rituals.

There are several tiers of Blood Altar, which increase in size and power – this is Tier 5.

You start by crafting a Blood Altar, Sacrificial Orb, and a Weak Blood Orb. You'll use these materials to make upgrades to your altars and orbs, gather more life essence for your altar and Soul Network, and create magical tokens like sigils for creating infinite water, flying, fast mining and farming, and more. As you perfect your tactic for gathering and storing life essence, you'll be able to perform more powerful (and expensive) rites and rituals. The Ritual of Magnetism pulls up ores in the ground (in a certain range) without you having to do any digging!

The Sigil of the Phantom Bridge creates a temporary black bridge beneath you as you walk.

The magic you use with Botania is probably the most cheerful of the magical mods. It's based on magical flower petals. But don't be fooled – the Botania magic is also powerful, and it is a complex and engaging mod. In Botania, you work with an energy called Mana, which you get from special mystical flowers.

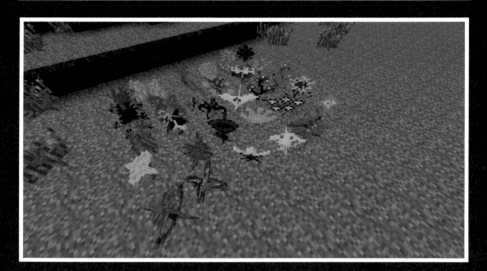

The Botania mod adds a variety of highly detailed and colourful flowers to use in your magic.

You gather the Mana from your flowers in a Mana Pool, which you then use to craft new items. Or you can distribute the Mana with special mechanisms to your Runic Altar, where you can create even more unique items.

Magic flowers generate Mana, which can be sent to collect in a Mana Pool.

Start by creating the guide book, the Lexica Botania, by crafting a book with a sapling together. This will give you a tutorial and information on everything you can do with Botania magic. Also, shift right-click on a Botania object with the Lexica to get more information about that object.

You can use the Runic Altar to craft new magical items using Mana as a source of power.

Morph doesn't bring a system of magic to Minecraft, but it does give you one awesome magical ability. With Morph, whenever you kill a mob, you gain the power to transform into that creature. You'll look like that creature and move like it too. Kill a bat and you'll be able to fly, kill a spider and you can float up walls. Use the left and right bracket keys to open up the menu to choose which creature you want to look like!

cappymiller

Grass Block
✓ Currently Harvestable
Effective Tool : Shovel
Minecraft

WildHorse

Mouse

Kitty

Villager

Duck

The Morph mod gives you the ability to morph into any creature you have killed. Select one from your list and you'll change into their size and be able to move like that creature.

CHAPTER 6

THE TECH MODS

Minecraft tech is all about crafting: bigger, better, and faster. There are machines to automate tasks like farming, chopping trees, and even breeding animals. There are pipes so you can transfer items, liquids, and energy. And there are storage systems that can hold so much more than a double chest. So forget mining with your enchanted diamond pickaxe. How would you like a quarry to dig out a 25x25 hole to bedrock, remove all the ores, and then smelt and sort them for you?

A basic ore-processing and energy set-up in a skyblock: cobble is turned into lava, which Dynamos convert into energy that is sent to power ore-crushers and sifters, which is smelted into ingots and packaged into blocks.

Like all the top mods in Minecraft, these tech mods have been well thought out and balanced by their creators. Balanced means that you won't be an auto-diamond machine made from two logs that outputs hundreds of diamonds for you. You have to gather resources and do some complicated crafting in order to get the contraptions that are the most advanced and profitable.

Another key concept in the tech mods is energy. In vanilla Minecraft, the only energy you need is the wood, coal, lava, or blaze rods you put into your furnace to smelt metals and cook food. High tech machines in these mods need much more power — power from generators, steam turbines, windmills, solar panels, and even nuclear reactors. (And you'll have to build them!)

There are three main types of Minecraft power:

- **Minecraft Joules (MJ)**: Used primarily by BuildCraft.

- **Redstone Flux (RF)**: Used by most mods.

- **Energy Units (EU)**: Used by IndustrialCraft 2 and its add-ons.

As a beginner, what you need to know about energy is that occasionally a machine from one mod will have difficulty being powered with a generator from another mod. Thermal Expansion's energy conduits will transfer between MJ and RF, and there are some mods that provide power converters. The easiest way to avoid needing power conversion is to use power generators and contraptions from the same mod.

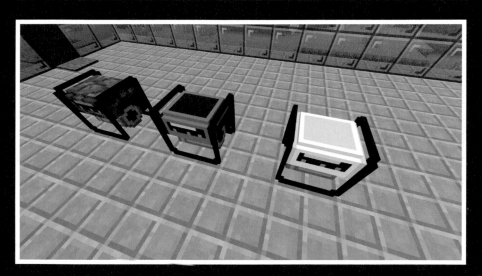

The Extra Utilities mod provides generators good for early game power, including the Survivalist Generator (vanilla fuel), the Ender Generator (Ender Pearls), and the Culinary Generator (various foods, including zombie brains).

These technical mods can have some very complicated mechanics behind them, and you can find endless discussions online at forums like reddit.com and the Minecraft forum about the ins and outs of their capabilities, efficiencies, conversions, and more. However, you can get started easily with all of these mods and pretty much do whatever you need to without getting bogged down in the details. And if you ARE into details, there are lots available for you!

BuildCraft

Authors: CovertJaguar, buildcraftchildsplay

BuildCraft is a long-standing, widely used, engineering-focused mod. It provides a number of machines for gathering and managing large quantities of resources, such as a quarry for mining, a pump to get and transfer liquids (like oil), a refinery to process your oil, and more. There are a variety of pipes to use for different tasks, and robots for planting, harvesting, shovelling, chopping trees, and more. Pipes in BuildCraft are see-through, so you can see your little blocks of cobble, dirt, ores, and more travelling to their destinations.

BuildCraft adds oil geysers throughout your world, and you can use the oil to power your factories.

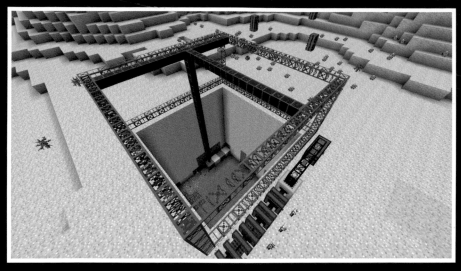

A BuildCraft quarry will dig straight down to bedrock for you and pump out the blocks it mines.

The BuildCraft MJ power comes from engines: from low-power Redstone Engines to the most powerful Combustion Engines that need a liquid fuel. Beware: the Combustion Engines can also explode, if you don't handle them carefully.

Thermal Expansion Series

Authors: TeamCoFH, KingLemming, jadedcat, ZeldoKavira

Designed initially to work as machines to complement BuildCraft, Thermal Expansion has grown to be a robust must-have tech mod in itself. You'll want to grab all three mods in the series: Thermal Expansion (machines, power, storage), Thermal Dynamics (transport pipes), and Thermal Foundation (a requirement for the others, this provides resources like ores).

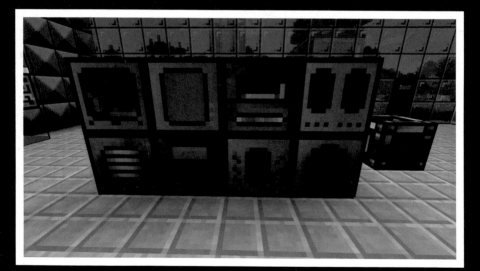

Thermal Expansion machines are very popular for their ore and material processing.

While BuildCraft helps gather resources like oil and rocks, Thermal Expansion machines help process ores and materials. A Redstone Furnace can smelt faster than a vanilla furnace, and an Induction Smelter can combine ores and materials into alloys. A Pulverizer will crush ores (and more), a Magma Crucible melts stuff, and a Fluid Transposer will take fluids and insert them into special containers. The machines are all upgradeable: a base crafting component – a machine frame – comes in four levels. The base level allows you to start making these machines while you still don't have many resources. As you gather more and more exotic items and resources (from the Nether and elsewhere), you can upgrade to more powerful machines. There are a variety of power generators called Dynamos, energy cells that act like power backups, plus pipes for transporting liquids, items, and energy. It's all terribly good fun, as you learn to hook all these together, amass crates and chests of resources, and craft your jetpack to fly around the Nether.

Minefactory Reloaded
- -

Authors: Skyboy026, TeamCoFH

Minefactory Reloaded (MFR) adds machines to help automate a lot of Minecraft tasks, such as fishing, planting, fertilizing, harvesting, milking, shearing, animal slaughter, and even enchanting. In general, the machines work on a single block in front of them, and you craft upgrades to insert into the machine so that they cover a wider area.

You can use two machines to make a very easy mob farm and grinder. First, you can catch a mob with a safari net and place the safari net in an auto-spawner. With power, the auto-spawner will spawn out the same type of mobs, then the mob grinder will kill the spawned mobs and collect their drops.

MFR also adds rubber trees and the processing of rubber into plastic and plastic sheets for crafting its machines. Other materials MFR adds are liquid meat, pink slime, sludge, and sewage.

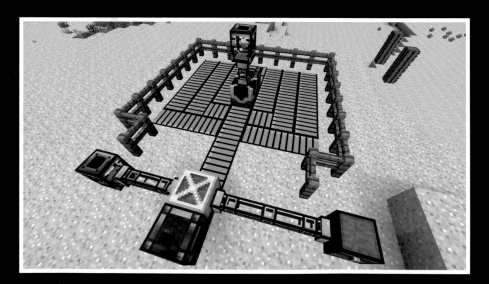

An MFR auto-spawner and grinder can make setting up mob farms easy.

Applied Energistics 2

Authors: AlgorithmX2, Cisien, thatsIch, fireball1725, akarso

Applied Energistics 2 (AE2) is an amazing mod that takes the concept of translating matter to energy and back again, and transforms crafting and storage. With AE2, you can transfer your material resources, from apples to zombie flesh, into "energy equivalents" and store them on computer-like hard drives called ME (Material Energy) drives. Building an ME network allows you to input and output resources at a distance, and a crafting monitor lets you craft and access resources from your drives on the network. Add a crafting CPU (Central Processing Unit), a few other gadgets, lots of power, and you can direct your crafting terminal to autocraft 100 pistons for you in about a minute. Nice. The mod's visuals are also beautifully designed and animated.

An AE2 setup for an ME network includes an ME controller, an ME drive with disks, crafting CPUs, a molecular assembler, and various monitors.

JABBA

Authors: ProfMobius, taelnia

If there's one thing the tech mods give you, it's tons and tons of resources — wood from automated tree farms, bones and mob drops from mob grinders, and blocks of metals from mining and smelting operations. Until you get your ME system up and running, you're going to need ways to store this stuff, and a hundred wooden chests is a lot to deal with. Here's where JABBA (Just Another Better Barrel Attempt) comes in. JABBA lets you create cheap barrels that will hold 64 stacks of a single item. You can upgrade the barrels to hold tons more by adding Structural Upgrades to upgrade slots, and then Storage Upgrades in the new slots. You can use a JABBA Dolly to move barrels (and regular chests) around without dropping their contents. And you can also add special upgrades, like redstone and hopper functionality.

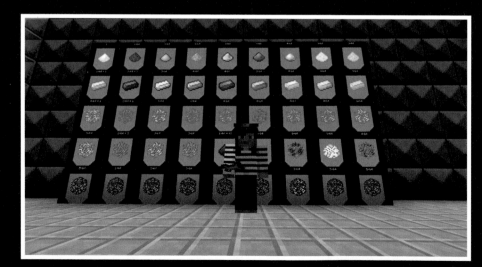

JABBA barrels can hold at minimum 64 stacks of a single item and be upgraded from there.

Other Tech Mods of Note:

These aren't the only great tech mods. Other mods you should seriously consider playing around with are:

- **IndustrialCraft2 (IC2):** Automation and factories.

- **Forestry:** Farming tech, with an emphasis on trees and bees you can cultivate into unique species.

- **Railcraft:** An in-depth overhaul of rails and carts.

- **ComputerCraft:** Adds computers and programmable robots called turtles.

- **EnderIO:** Ore processing, resource transportation, power.

- **ProjectRed:** Adds new functionality and gadgets for you to create your original contraptions.

- **Big Reactors:** If you just can't get enough power, go nuclear.

One of the smaller reactors from the mod Big Reactors. It uses yellorium as fuel, is cooled by gelid cryotheum, and outputs power and cyanite as waste.

CHAPTER 7

MODS FOR BUILDERS

There's a bounty of mods that can help Minecraft architects, interior designers, and mapmakers perfect their creations. Some add to the blocks you can use to decorate and build with; others make the act of building large structures much, much easier.

Chisel 2

Authors: TheCricket26, Drullkus

Chisel 2 adds many new textures to existing blocks. In the same way vanilla sandstone has several looks (chiselled, plain, etc.), Chisel 2 lets you choose different looks for many blocks. You have to craft the chisel tool and right-click it to open up a GUI (Graphic User Interface). Just insert the block you want to see variants of, then pull out your choice.

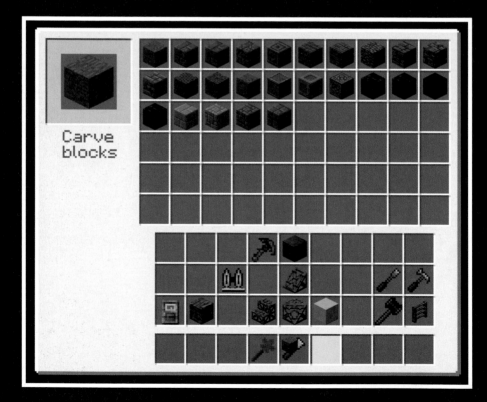

Place the Chisel 2 chisel and right-click to open the Chisel 2 GUI. Here you can drag a block and see the other styles Chisel 2 can transform it into.

Carpenter's Blocks

Authors: Syntaxial, Mineshopper

This mod adds the Carpenter's Block, a kind of frame. You can add any texture from a second block, making the first block look just like the second. This gets interesting when there is more than one type of Carpenter's Block. Some will let you create angled blocks (rather than square). There's the wedge slope, the stair, the ladder, the door, and more. Many of these Carpenter's Blocks can be turned to multiple positions and have several base textures to choose from.

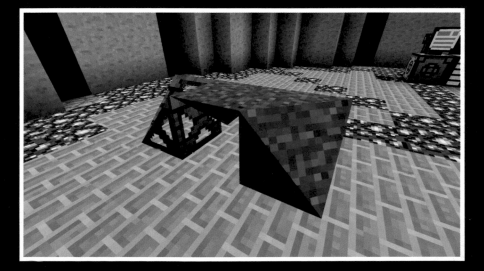

Carpenter's Blocks adds several blocks that have angles. You can cycle through how they are positioned using a Carpenter's Hammer, and apply a texture from another block to them. These angled blocks have been textured with a block of grass.

Use a Carpenter's Hammer to change the style of a Carpenter's Door, then right-click any block on the door to change its texture. Here, the lapis block was used to create the blue door.

DecoCraft2

Authors: RazzleberryFox, taelnia, ProfMobius, lukitiki, Davexx100

Tired of fiddling around with stairs, fences, and slabs to make large clunky furniture? Struggle no more – add the mod DecoCraft2 and you'll have hundreds of objects to decorate your base, from grand pianos and laptops to Christmas trees, picnic baskets, canopy beds, and more.

Here are just a few of the kitchen-themed items from DecoCraft.

BiblioCraft

Author: JDSinclair

BiblioCraft adds decorative objects to Minecraft as well, centred on a library theme. You can now replace all those oak bookshelves with spruce or any other wood, add chairs, desks, lamps, picture frames, and shelves.

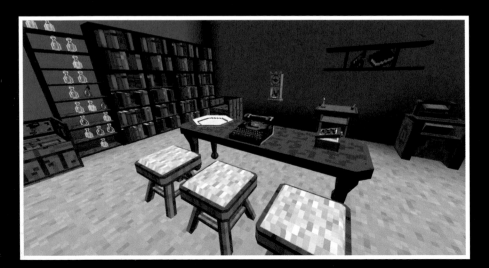

BiblioCraft adds lots of book and office-related items, like typewriters and shelves.

Pam's HarvestCraft

Author: MatrexsVigil

Pam's HarvestCraft adds tons of crops, bushes, fruit trees, and food, including vegetarian options like soya milk and tofu. You don't have to limit yourself to steak, pork chops, and baked potatoes anymore. Pam's HarvestCraft has so many food options and recipes – there are even five types of doughnuts!

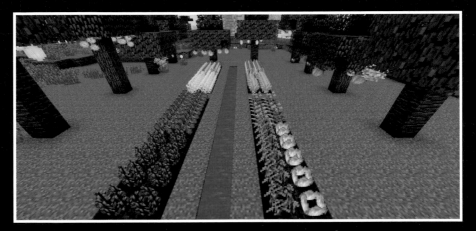

Create a garden of fruit and nut trees and really expand your home vegetable garden with Pam's HarvestCraft.

WorldEdit

Author: sk89q

WorldEdit is a mapmaking tool that lets you quickly create and destroy blocks in large numbers. You need to have Cheats enabled in your world in order for it to work. Although there is an Undo command, you can massively change your world with WorldEdit, so you do need to be careful!

Things you can do include:

- Quickly create cubes, spheres, circles, and more out of any block.

- Copy, paste, and rotate a set of blocks.

- Use terraforming brushes to add, replace, and smooth blocks.

- Fix water problems and drain and fill pools.

- Create a forest.

- Save a copied area as a schematic to load into other worlds.

There is a little bit of a learning curve to WorldEdit, and you can find detailed information on this mod's capabilities at the WorldEdit wiki at wiki.sk89q.com/wiki/WorldEdit.

If you want an earth bridge to stretch out over your sci-fi dune landscape, WorldEdit can make it happen in minutes.

CHAPTER 8

PLAYING WITH MODPACKS

So once you've downloaded a modpack, what happens next? In the modpack launcher, just click the name of the modpack you're starting, and a familiar Minecraft launcher open, which has all the settings configured for you to play. (If you play with a really large pack of mods, you may want to increase your memory setting to 4GB, as long as your system has at least 8GB RAM.) You then create a new world in pretty much the same way you do in vanilla Minecraft. Find out if you are playing with the Biomes O' Plenty mod. If you are, you will have to set the World Type of your new world to Biomes O' Plenty. And for the few modpacks that include a specific map to play with, you'll have to select that world type in the Play screen.

Starting in a Modded World

When you arrive in your world, just follow vanilla procedures to get started. Punch wood, make a crafting table and some beginning tools, and gather a little food. You'll also want to prepare a temporary and safe home base. Mobs are generally much more dangerous in modded Minecraft because many mods add new, more powerful mobs. (You'll also have lots of ways to better protect yourself!) Keep a look out for the Natura mod's berry bushes and apple trees from Biomes O' Plenty. These are a great early food source.

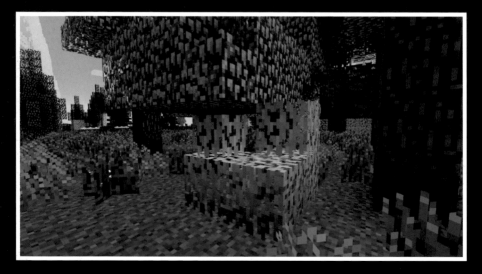

The Natura berry bushes and the apple trees from Biomes O' Plenty mods are a great early food source, if you have them.

Most modpacks include NEI or a similar mod, Too Many Items (TMI), to help manage your inventory. You can use NEI to look at which modpacks are installed and the items they provide. To see the mods installed, click **E** to open NEI, and then click the **Item Subsets** button to open different ways to explore the inventory. Click the **Mod** button to open up the list of mods, which you can scroll through. To see the objects and items added by a mod, type an at symbol (@) with the name of the mod, as in "@ Tinkers' Construct," in the NEI search box. The grid on the right will then show only the items from that modpack.

Use an inventory-management mod like NEI to see which mods are installed and the items they add.

One thing to be aware of: modpacks sometimes change recipes for modded objects, and items, and vanilla items. For instance, in the Regrowth modpack, the crafting table is made with two wood slabs and two planks. And this is why modpacks include the NEI mod, because NEI helps you find all the recipes. The reason modpack authors do this is to tweak the rate at which you advance through learning and crafting new objects and technologies. They are balancing out the gameplay so you have to work a little more or explore a little more than normal.

You will also usually have JourneyMap or a similar mini-map mod installed. If you travel around, use the waypoint tool (press **B** in JourneyMap) to mark spots you'd like to come back to, like a ravine or a village, and your home base.

Once you've established yourself with some basic tools, a food source, and maybe a small animal farm, your next goal is usually to start amassing resources, like metals. If Tinkers' Construct mod is included, you'll want to create the four Tinkers' Construct blocks for crafting tools:

- **A Stencil Table:** To make stencils for tool parts.

- **A Stencil Chest:** To store these next to the part table.

- **The Parts Table:** Where you construct tool and weapon parts using the stencils and a permitted material. Place the Stencil Chest next to this to access the chests inventory.

- **The Tool Forge:** Where you combine two or more parts to create the final weapon or tool.

From left to right, the four Tinkers' Construct blocks you need to craft tools and weapons: Stencil Table, Stencil Chest, Parts Table, and Tool Forge.

The Tool Forge is the advanced version of the Tool Station, which you will usually create first, because it is cheaper to create. However, it doesn't include some of the advanced tools. When you have enough iron to spare, create the Tool Forge, so you can create a hammer. The hammer will mine out 3x3 tunnels. This single tool changes mining from being time-consuming to great fun. And an excavator does the same for dirt and sand. And if you don't already have them, make the Tinkers' Construct guide books, Materials and You, Volumes 1 and 2, and Might Smelting, to help you with materials choices. At the beginning, before you have many resources, you can make tools with cobble – these are cheap to repair. Once you are able to make or gather obsidian, try to make your tools out of alumite – this alloy you create with the smeltery will let you mine the two top metal ores in the Nether: cobalt and ardite.

Early on, explore to find the villages in your area. If your modpack includes Tinkers' Construct, a village can spawn with a small smeltery ready for you to start using. I'll often look for a village right at the start, to help me get started with some resources. If you have a walled village, like those that the Witchery mod adds, it is usually pretty easy to secure the village walls and start playing with relatively little danger.

Something else to watch out for when starting to play mods is multiblock structures. These are structures built out of many blocks, like Tinkers' Construct smelteries. These multiblock structures don't become activated until they are built properly. Many mods that have multiblock structures include in-game books of instructions that appear when you spawn for the first time. If you are ever stuck, and you haven't found a book about the mod in your inventory or in NEI, a great place to start looking for information is the FTB wiki, at ftbwiki.org.

If the Witchery mod is installed in your modpack, a walled village is a great place to make your first base. Just close up the village entrances and light the village to help secure it.

Starting in a HQM World

A HQM modpack includes the mod Hardcore Questing Mode. With this, the modpack developer has set up quests for you to follow, and you'll typically spawn with a quest book that you use to figure out your next task. In these worlds, follow the first quests – they will set you up with what you initially need to survive. Also note the word "Hardcore". In Minecraft, this means you have one life to live in the world – once you die, it's all over. However, most HQM modpacks give you several lives and opportunities along the way to earn more.

One great way to start a specific modpack is to play along with a YouTuber that you like. Many Minecraft YouTubers have Let's Play series based on a modpack. You can see what they are up to, follow along, get inspired, copy, and learn. I'd recommend looking at direwolf20's modded, single-player Let's Play Season 7 series, using his own modpack called Direwolf20. You can download this modpack with the Curse Launcher. Every ten episodes or so, direwolf20 posts links with the YouTube episode so you can download and play with his current world. Opening his world in your modded launcher means that you can see exactly how he is putting everything together. For an entertaining look at how creative you can get with a modpack, take a look at Etho's Modded Minecraft series by Ethoslab.

direwolf20's Let's Play single-player YouTube series is a great way to follow along and play with an experienced modded Minecraft player. Here, direwolf20 contends with giant lookalikes in the Twilight Forest, using a pink slime crossbow.

The Agrarian Skies 1

Author: jadedcat

Because mods and modpacks can be very overwhelming – adding thousands of items, new types of gameplay, new interfaces for new machines, and more, I highly recommend starting out with one specific modpack: Agrarian Skies 1 (AS1). It is one of the most popular – if not THE most popular – modpacks available.

The premise of Agrarian Skies 1 is that the world has been almost completely destroyed by monsters. A group of godlike mages have chosen you to try and rebuild the world starting from almost nothing on a tiny island. While the mages will help you, they will also ask for things in return. As it happens, they ask for a lot of things in return.

Agrarian Skies 1 is a great modpack to start with for several reasons. First, it has a fun storyline and includes the HQM questing system. The questing system gives you challenges to complete and rewards when you complete them, which will give you an incentive for following all the quests.

Second, the pack is simply a great introduction to playing mods – it includes a number of the most popular and helps you start to find your way through them.

Third, Agrarian Skies 1 is a modded skyblock map. A skyblock map is an empty world with a little block of Minecraft land floating by itself in the sky (see the chapter opening image). If you fall off the edge, you will die in the Void. On the bright side, it is much easier to control hostile mobs spawning.

And finally, because the Agrarian Skies 1 modpack is so popular, it is fairly easy to find help and ideas on gameplay if you get stuck. Minecrafters have compiled lists of tips for Agrarian Skies 1, and many people have played it.

Note: While AS1 is based on Minecraft 1.6.4, the modpacks and skyblock setting prevent the pack from seeming out of date, especially if you are new to mods. There is also a new Agrarian Skies modpack, Agrarian Skies 2. Many of the same concepts of the first Agrarian Skies apply to the second.

A few forums to look at for help are the AS1 tips and tricks lists on reddit.com and at Curse's FTB forum. However, you may find some spoilers here on gameplay elements that would otherwise surprise you.

- reddit.com/r/feedthebeast/comments/231p8t/ agrskies_agrarian_skies_tips_and_tricks/
- forum.feed-the-beast.com/threads/ spoiler-alert-agrarian-skies-hints-tips-secrets.44516/

Starting Agrarian Skies 1

1. Use the FTB launcher to download and install Agrarian Skies 1. Before starting the modpack, you'll also need to install the special map that comes with it. In the FTB launcher, click **Maps & Textures**. Press the **Maps** button to open the Maps screen. In the list of maps on the left, click **Agrarian Skies Default Map (v.1)** and then click **Install Map** to install the map.

2. In the FTB launcher, with Agrarian Skies 1 selected in the list of modpacks, click **Launch** to start the game. Click **Singleplayer** when the Minecraft screen opens. In the Select World Screen, select **Home Sweet Home T** and click **Play Selected World**. You'll arrive inside a single room house floating in the sky on some clay blocks. There are often update announcements from mod authors on the opening screen. You can ignore these, as your FTB launcher will update the modpack when necessary.

You start inside a tiny house on a skyblock in Agrarian Skies facing a chest.

3. In your inventory is a thin brown book called the quest book. This is what guides you through the mods. Right-click the quest book to open it, and read or play the introduction. When you've finished the introduction, click **Click Here** to start.

4. The quest book opens to show you the list of quest areas (there are multiple quests in each area). You'll see the number of lives you have left in the top right. This is a Hardcore map, meaning you only have a limited number of lives to play the map. However, quests along the way will help you gather more lives, and if you make it past the first week, you should be fine. The "Party" heading only applies if you are playing in a multiplayer setting, so you can ignore that. And under the "Quests" heading, you'll see your progress.

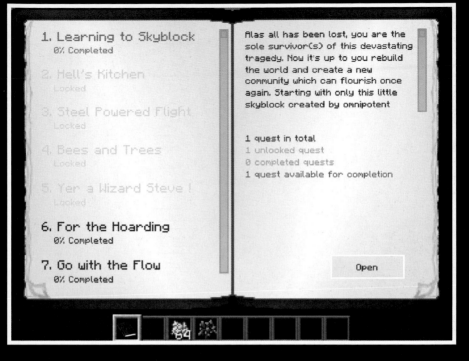

The quest book contents page lists the quest areas and shows your progress.

5. Open the chest in your house and notice there is no food. Not a scrap. You're going to have to be very careful to avoid hunger-inducing tasks (like jumping up blocks) until you sort out your food situation. You are going to have to grow oak trees and eat apples – luckily there is a fair amount of bonemeal you can use to get your trees started. (Also, take a look under your single block of dirt.)

6. You can get started on quests right away, as they help you survive the first few days. Select **1. Learning to Skyblock**, and on the right page, read the introduction to this area. Then, click **Open** to open the quest list. The quests appear as hexagonal buttons. They flash when they are ready to be played.

7. At first there is only one quest under Learning to

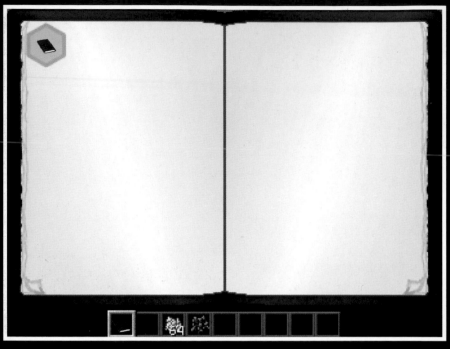

Each quest has a hexagonal button.

Skyblock, but more will appear as you go on. Click the **Using the Book** quest icon to open the quest page and read your instructions. On the right page, you'll see what you have to provide or do in order to complete the quest. On the left is a description of the quest, followed by a list of the quest goals (there may be more than one), and a list of the rewards you will get for completing the quest. Sometimes you will have to choose between different options for your reward.

8. For the first quest, you must craft one block of planks, so you'll want to grow an oak tree, punch it down, and make a block of oak planks.

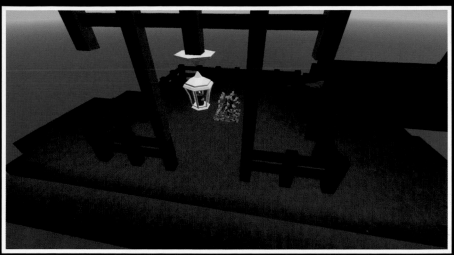

Plant your oak on the block of dirt outside.

9. Open the quest book again to your quest page. On the right, you'll see that you've completed the task. On the left, the **Claim Reward** button has activated, so click that to get your rewards.

On the left page, click **Claim Reward** once you've finished the task.

10. Right-click a page to return to the previous page in the quest book. This takes you to the list of quests for Learning to Skyblock. You'll see that the icon for your completed quest is no longer flashing and two more quests have been unlocked. (If you ever see that a completed quest is still flashing and purple, this is because you can still claim a reward for it.)

11. After the first task, the quest book shows you other ways to complete tasks for the quest book. You can simply follow the quest book from here on. Once you've resolved your food situation, you can start taking breaks from the quest book to improve your base or spend extra time on one mod or set of machines as you like.

Here are a few additional tips to help you manage your first week or so:

- If, for some reason, your first oak tree doesn't give you saplings, don't despair. You can submit items crafted with another wood type for quests until you get more oak seeds with later activities.

- When you set up the quest delivery system, right-click with the hopper to a side of the QDS block. You must use a pick to remove the hopper.

- Build a tree farm of at least nine trees or more.

- Cooked silkworm is a decent food source.

- You can cook food in a pan without a furnace.

- If you are given the option of a slime sapling for a reward (or a slime bucket), choose it over anything else. Slime is hard to come by.

- When given a choice between a reward bag and another item, look in NEI to see how difficult it would be to make or get that item. You'll often find that the reward item is relatively easy to get, so you can feel good about taking that reward bag. Some reward bags have great stuff in them, others, not so much.

- Mobs don't spawn on bottom slabs (the slab that aligns with the bottom of a regular block). You can conserve wood and stop mobs from spawning by extending your base on half slabs.

- Make charcoal for torches.

- Try to gather and always keep several saplings of each type.

- Don't use up all the bonemeal you start out with; you will need some to make porcelain clay.

- Because there's nowhere for mobs to spawn, they'll spawn quickly wherever they can. This means you can build a simple mob farm of just an enclosed room some 20 blocks away from your base. Leave just a half-block-high space where the mob's feet will be so you can kill them and collect their drops.

To fish in the tiny pool, stand in one corner, and look straight up to cast the line. The line will usually come down into the pool and start bobbing. If it doesn't, try again.

You can also find loads of YouTube series on playing Agrarian Skies 1. Popular Minecraft YouTubers that have AS1 series include Generikb, direwolf20, Hypnotizd, and Yogscast.

CHAPTER 9

STARTING FTB INFINITY EVOLVED

FTB Infinity Evolved has a bit of everything! It has the latest mods for magic, tech, exploration, and fun, all tweaked by the FTB team to work well together. It is also a bit of a monster, meaning it has LOADS of mods. You will need to have enough computer memory to assign 2GB or more to running it. It is not a HQM modpack, so you won't have any guidance during the game. Here are steps to installing and starting your world with this modpack.

1. Download and install the Curse Launcher at http://beta. cursevoice.com/games/minecraft.

2. In the Curse Launcher, click **Browse FTB Modpacks**.

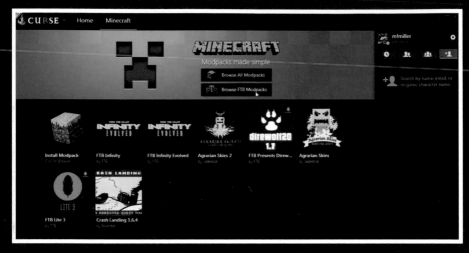

3. Locate FTB Infinity Evolved in the list.

4. Click the **Install** button on the FTB Infinity Evolved icon to install the modpack. The Curse Launcher will display the installation progress.

5. Once the modpack is installed, make sure you have enough RAM (computer memory) allocated. At the top right of the Curse Launcher, click the gear icon and click **Settings** on the pull-down menu.

6. In the Curse Settings screen, select Minecraft on the left panel to open the Minecraft settings.

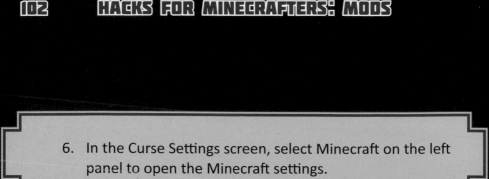

7. In the Java Settings section, make sure that the memory allocation amount is set to at least 2GB (on the far right of the slider here, it is set at 3GB). You can drag the circle on the slider to a new position. I set mine to 4GB.

8. Click **Save** to save your settings to return to the Curse Launcher.

9. Now that the modpack is installed and your memory settings are set, mouse over the FTB Infinity Evolved Icon on the launcher. The icon will change to include an orange Play button. Click the **Play** button.

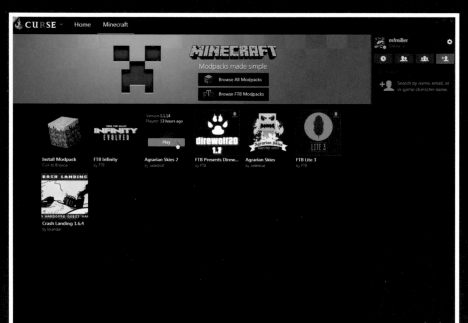

10. The Curse Launcher will then open up the Minecraft launcher, already configured to work with the modpack. Click **Start** in the Minecraft launcher.

Minecraft Launcher 1.6.48

Update Notes | Launcher Log | Profile Editor

Minecraft News

Official links:

Minecraft.net
Minecraft Realms
Minecraft on Facebook
Merchandise

Minecraft Realms survey

Update: Thanks everyone who participated! We have now closed the survey

Bug tracker
Account Support

~~Hello builders!~~

~~We're curious on what you know about various servers and how much you know about Realms. If we could have a minute or three of your time answering some questions, that would be great. Your answers will be super helpful for us to continue exploring new ideas and developing our services. Here's the link:~~

Mojang on Twitter
Support on Twitter

Try our other games!

Thank you! <3

Minecraft 1.8.8

We have released Minecraft version 1.8.8 to fix some security issues and improved

Profile: FTB Infinity ▾

New Profile | Edit Profile

Play

Welcome, **cappymiller**
Ready to play Minecraft forge-10.13.4.1448

Switch User

11. Next, the mod-loading screen will open, showing the progress in loading all of the mods.

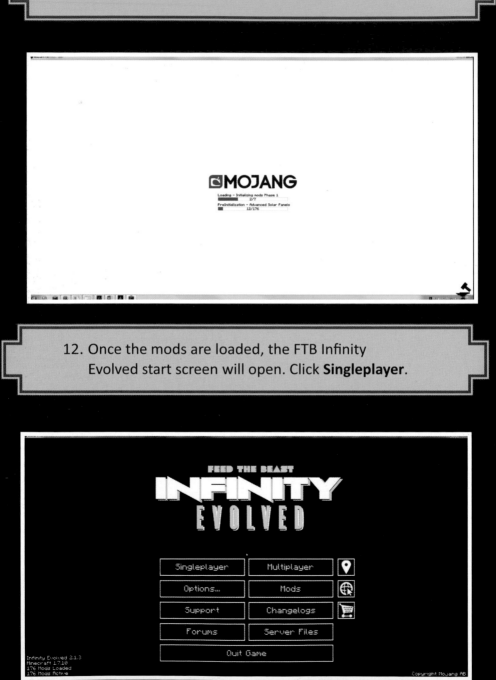

12. Once the mods are loaded, the FTB Infinity Evolved start screen will open. Click **Singleplayer**.

13. The Select World screen will open. Click **Create New World**.

14. If you've never played the modpack before, the Biomes O' Plenty splash screen opens to advise you on how to start a Biomes O' Plenty world. We'll do that now. Click **OK** to proceed.

Biomes O' Plenty uses a custom worldtype for its biomes. It may be enabled by clicking the 'World Type' button under 'More World Options' until it displays 'Biomes O' Plenty'.

The worldtype can be used on servers by changing the 'level-type' in server.properties to 'BIOMESOP' (without quotes)

15. In the Create New World screen that opens, click **More World Options**.

Create New World

World Name

New World

Will be saved in: New World

Game Mode Survival

Search for resources, crafting, gain
levels, health and hunger

More World Options...

Create New World   Cancel

16. In the World Options screen, click the **World Type: Default** button several times to cycle through the World Type options. Stop when you see **World Type: Biomes O' Plenty**.

Create New World

Seed for the World Generator

Leave blank for a random seed

Generate Structures: ON   World Type: Biomes O' Plenty

Villages, dungeons etc

Allow Cheats: OFF   Bonus Chest: OFF

Commands like /gamemode, /xp

Done

Create New World   Cancel

17. If you like, add a seed in the Seed for the World Generator text box. This can be any string of characters, and it is used to create your world. Defining a seed means you can easily share it with others. If your seed generates a great world, your friends may want to use the same seed for their world. Here, I've typed in "a nest of chickens" for the seed. Let's see what that gets us. Click **Done** to return to the first Create New World screen.

Create New World

Seed for the World Generator

    a nest of chickens_

Leave blank for a random seed

Generate Structures: ON   World Type: Biomes O' Plenty

Villages, dungeons etc.

Allow Cheats: OFF   Bonus Chest: OFF

Commands like /gamemode, /xp

Done .

Create New World   Cancel

18. Now type in a name for your world (I've used the seed for the name – "a nest of chickens" – which will help me remember the seed). Click **Create New World** to begin your game!

Create New World

World Name

a nest of chickens_

Will be saved in: a nest of chickens

Game Mode Survival

Search for resources, crafting, gain levels, health and hunger

More World Options...

Create New World   Cancel

19. Congratulations! You've made it to your modded world! And, with my seed, I've landed in a swamp, with a couple of books in my hand! The books are guides to Tinkers' Construct mod, so I will hold on to them.

Playing On

Just like in vanilla Minecraft, my first goals in this FTB modpack (and any modpack, really) are tools, weapons, shelter, and food. There are willow trees in the swamp, and these are just as good as oak for making a crafting table and wooden tools. They're also one of my favourite trees, with a nice greyish-green colour. Time to punch wood and craft a wood axe, shovel, pick, and sword.

Now, for a look about. This spawn looks pretty good because we are close to a magical forest, which will help later with playing some of the magical mods.

You can tell this is a Magical Forest Biome because of the magical, blue-leafed Silverwood tree.

There should be plenty of food around, beyond the meat you can get from cows, chickens, sheep, and pigs. I should be able to find berries from Natura berry bushes, as well as fruit trees, plants, and "gardens" added by the mod Pam's HarvestCraft. Breaking these gardens will give you plant items, many of which you can eat. There's a Berry Garden, Desert Garden, Gourd Garden, Grass Garden, Ground Garden, Herb Garden, Leafy Garden, Mushroom Garden, Stalk Garden, Textile Garden, Tropical Garden, and Water Garden.

Look out for Pam's HarvestCraft gardens, like this Stalk Garden. You can break it to get eggplants (aubergines), beans, peppers, and more. You can eat these vegetables or place them in a crafting grid to make seeds to grow your own vegetables. You can also search in NEI for the recipes that use them to make special foods, like Eggplant Parm.

Here's a cow with a hat. The Hats mod adds random and strange hats to mobs. You have to kill the mob to get its hat. Once you do, press H to open the Hat settings screen and select the hat you want to wear.

First I like to find a village. Villages are one of my favourite things in large modpacks because different mods add new buildings, resources, walls, and villager traders. Plus, they look really cool. Villages also spawn more frequently in the Infinity modpacks so it doesn't take as long to find a village. So now that I have my first tools, I'm going to explore and gather food as I go. I especially want to kill sheep for wool, to make a bed, so I'll be able to sleep and avoid the monsters for now.

You will find hobgoblins as you explore. They are a neutral mob so they won't attack you unless you attack them first.

I find a village not too far from spawn, at X=677, Z=737. The Witchery mod adds sentry guards who will attack any mobs. However, they aren't foolproof. Until I secure the village, by improving walls and lighting, I will need to fall asleep at sunset to stop the mob. But I am home, free! It's time to start playing around with mods. You'll want to first explore Tinkers' Construct for creating better weapons and tools and start mining for the best ores. Once you have better weapons, the mods you play with are up to you. I usually start with the tech mods. I concentrate on mining and improving my resource-gathering with the machines from the Thermal Expansion and MineFactory Reloaded mods. Once I have tons of resources (metals, gems, and more) pouring in, I build advanced storage and crafting with Applied Energistics. However, an equally valid way to start is with the magical mods. These can have you up and running with super resources and gear quickly, too, and I may try this on my next modded world!

I found a nice big village, with lots of the buildings added by mods: an Apiarist's house with goodies to get started playing with bees, an Agricraft greenhouse, a Tinkers' house, a smeltery, and more.

To explore the FTB Infinity Evolved mods further, visit the FTB wikis, which cover the mods the FTB team use in their modpacks. These are my go-to sources, along with using Google for specific questions. There's the unofficial FTB wiki, at ftbwiki. org, and the official FTB wiki, at ftb.gamepedia.com. There are also some helpful Getting Started tutorials at ftb.gamepedia. com/Getting_Started_(Main). You can find links to these sites and more at my website, meganfmiller.com. See you there!

APPENDIX

To start working with mods individually, you will need to have intermediate to advanced computer skills, including:

a) Knowing what zipped files are and how to work with them.

b) Knowing how to navigate your file system.

c) Knowing how to find a mod online, and making sure you have read all the requirements for a mod and instructions for installing it.

d) Understanding that some mods may conflict with each other, especially mods that are modifying the same types of activities in Minecraft (for example, two mods that modify Minecraft villagers).

e) Making backups of your Minecraft worlds.

f) Being able to troubleshoot crashes and incompatibilities using online resources, such as the Minecraft wiki, the Minecraft Forum, relevant mod forums, and Reddit forums.

Installing a Mod with MultiMC 5

1. To install MultiMC, go to the MultiMC website at https://multimc.org and download the application that is right for your platform (Windows, Mac, or Linux). A zipped folder will download.

2. Once the download is finished, open the zipped folder and drag the folder that is inside – labelled MultiMC – to your hard drive. Since there isn't a regular installer

for the program, you'll need to remember where you drag this folder to. The location that you drag it to will be the location where the program runs from.

3. Then, to run the MultiMC program, open the MultiMC folder and double-click the MultiMC.exe file.

4. Next, you will want to change your settings in MultiMC. First, click the **Accounts** button at the top right, and select **Manage Accounts**. This opens up the Settings dialog box to the Accounts tab. (You can also click the **Change Settings** button in the top menu bar.)

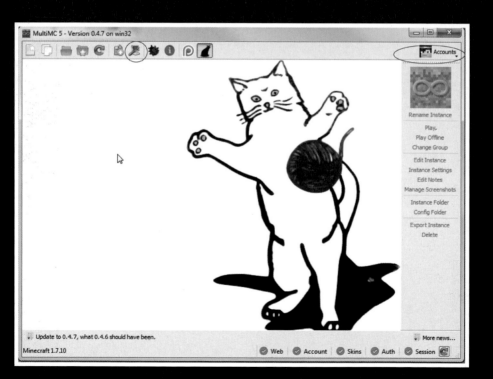

To change settings, click the **Change Settings** button in the menu bar (circled in red). You can also click **Accounts** in the top right and then select **Manage Accounts**.

5. In the Accounts tab, add your Minecraft profile (your email/username and password).
6. In the Java tab, change the default maximum memory specified in the Maximum memory allocation box. Mods, and especially modpacks, use quite a bit more computer memory than vanilla Minecraft. You shouldn't set Maximum memory allocation to more than half of your computer memory and, if possible, set this to 1GB (1024 MB) or 2 GB (2048 MB).

Mods take up more memory so you will usually want to change the maximum memory allocation in the Java tab. You can use the arrows in the spin box to change the memory allocation.

7. In the Minecraft window, you can change the size of the window that the Minecraft game starts in. If you want the game to run full-screen, select the **Start Minecraft maximized** check button.
8. Close the Settings dialog box.
9. Create a new instance (essentially a copy of the Minecraft game that you will use chosen mods with) by clicking the **New Instance** button on the left of the top menu bar.
10. In the **New Instance** dialog box, name your instance. Here, I've called this instance "First".

In the New Instance dialog box, you can name your instance, create or select a group to put it in, and specify which version of Minecraft you are using. Instead of working with vanilla Minecraft, you can choose to use a downloaded modpack instead.

11. Under **Vanilla Minecraft**, click the **...** button and then select **1.7.10** as the version of Minecraft to use and click **OK**. (Minecraft 1.7.10 currently has the most number of mods available for it.)

12. Click **OK** to close the New Instance dialog box. The program will update to download the right files for the Minecraft version you selected.

13. Right-click the icon for the instance, and select **Edit Instance**.

14. In the Edit Instance dialog box, click the **Install Forge** button. This will open up a window to confirm which version of Forge to install. Keep the recommended Forge version (this will have a star next to it) and click **OK**.

Version	Branch
Forge 10.13.4.1481	1.7.10
Forge 10.13.4.1472	1.7.10
Forge 10.13.4.1470	1.7.10
Forge 10.13.4.1469	1.7.10
Forge 10.13.4.1456	1.7.10
Forge 10.13.4.1452	1.7.10
Forge 10.13.4.1451	1.7.10
☆ Forge 10.13.4.1448	1.7.10
Forge 10.13.4.1447	1.7.10
Forge 10.13.4.1445	Recommended 1.10
Forge 10.13.3.1428	1.7.10
Forge 10.13.3.1424	1.7.10
Forge 10.13.3.1422	1.7.10
Forge 10.13.3.1420	1.7.10
Forge 10.13.3.1408	1.7.10

Select Forge version

Refresh　　　OK　　　Cancel

In the Select Forge version dialog box, the version of Forge that is recommended for you to use with the Minecraft version you selected will have a yellow star beside it.

15. Click **Close** to close the Edit Instance dialog box.

16. Open your central mods folder by clicking the blue folder with a gold star icon in the menu bar. This folder is a handy place to keep your downloaded mods, as MultiMC will look here first when you later add mods to an instance.

17. Next, download the mods you want to use to your central mods folder you opened in the previous step. WARNING: These downloaded mods will have to be compatible with the version of Forge and Minecraft you are using. Some mods also require you to install other mods (requirements). You will need to make sure to download and install any requirements. Two places to find mods are

    a. Curse: curse.com/mc-mods/minecraft

    b. The Minecraft Forum: minecraftforum.net/

18. I've downloaded the mod Not Enough Items and a required file, CodeChickenCore, from the mod author's site at chickenbones.net.

19. Once you have downloaded the mod you want, you'll need to add it to your instance. With your instance selected in the main MultiMC panel, click **Edit Instance** in the right panel.

20. Click the **Install Mods** button on the right. You can also click the **Loader Mods** tab on the left.

21. In the Loader mods tab, click the **Add** button on the right. This will open up your central MultiMC mods folder.

22. Select the mod or mods you want to add and click **Open**.

23. Click **Close** to close the Edit Instance dialog box.

24. You are now ready to play Minecraft with the mod(s) you have just added. Double-click the instance in the main panel to start your modded Minecraft game. If a

console window opens, you can minimize it or move this out of the way of your game window.

25. When your Minecraft game start window opens, you can start the game. To play your modded game at a later date, you'll have to open the MultiMC launcher again, and double-click your instance.

Your starting window will show what version of Minecraft you are using along with the version of Forge and the number of mods that are loaded and active. You can also click the Mods button to see a list of active mods.

Tip: If you are going to use a lot of different instances, you can create groups to organize your instances into. You can select or create a group when you first create an instance or by right-clicking an instance and selecting **Change Group** in the dropdown menu.